Kenny's Favorite Science Facts & Trivia
By Kenny 'K3' Rochon, III
and Daddy

ISBN: 978-1-64810-043-7

PRINTED IN THE UNITED STATES OF AMERICA

This is dedicated my Mom and Dad and Grandpa and Grandma Ruthann Aunt Lizy, Uncle Alex, Caroline, Stephanie, Uncle Stevie, Aunt Sharron, Matt Rochon, Andrew Rochon, Aunt Jen, Uncle Patrick, Kay Kay Herwig, Brendan Herwig.

To my friend Ally, Amelia, Anthony, Barbara, Beth, Cathy, Drake, Eddie, James, Jayden, Jonah, Nico, Tyson, and all my friends at school.

And to my teacher Mrs. Kalinock.

-Kenny

This is dedicated to my favorite people in the world. My son who lights up my life and inspires me to publish a book a year for him and my loving wife who is the best mother in the world to our son. Raising a child with love is the way to ultimately bring more smiles to the world.

Also, a special thanks to Carolyn Sheltraw for her help with layout, Tara Hannon for the front cover illustration. Al Granger for his hand in making another book (almost 200) a reality and a super fun book to help fund Kenny's education.

- Ken Rochon, Jr

BRANCHES of SCIENCE

Q: Scientist who studies outer space is called?
A: Astronomer

Q: Scientist who studies life is called?
A: Biologist

Q: Scientist who studies plants is called?
A: Botanist

Q: Scientist who studies atomic matter is called?
A: Chemist

Q: Scientist who studies rocks is called?
A: Cosmologist

Q: Scientist who studies insects is called?
A: Entomologist

Q: Scientist who studies rocks is called?
A: Geologist

Q: Scientist who studies water is called?
A: Hydrologist

Q: Scientist who studies ocean animals and plants is called?
A: Marine Biologist

Q: Scientist who studies weather is called?
A: Meteorologist

Q: Scientist who studies cancer is called?
A: Oncologist

Q: Scientist who studies energy and matter is called?
A: Physicist

Q: Scientist who studies human behavior is called?
A: Psychologist

Q: Scientist who studies
Animals is called?
A: Zoologist

INVENTORS

Q: The Nobel Peace Prize is one of the most prestigious awards in the field of science. The man behind the award – Alfred Noble invented what?
A: Dynamite

Q: Who invented the first car?
A: Karl Benz

Q: Who invented the first computer?
A: Charles Babbage

Q: Who invented the Credit Card Magnetic Strip?
A: Ron Klein

Q: Who invented the Electric Battery?
A: Alessandro Volta (1800)

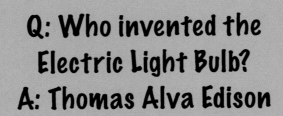

Q: Who invented the
Electric Light Bulb?
A: Thomas Alva Edison

Q: Who invented the
Printing Press?
A: Johannes Gutenberg (1450)

Q: Who invented scissors?
A: Leonardo da Vinci

Q: Who invented the Steam Engine?
A: Thomas Newcomen (1712)

Q: Who invented the telephone?
A: Alexander Graham Bell

Q: Who invented the first television?
A: Philo Farnsworth

Q: Who invented the Internet
(World Wide Web)?
A: Tim Berners-Lee

SCIENTISTS

Q: Who spoke 8 languages, known for designing the alternating-current (AC) electric system, the 'Tesla coil' used in radio technology, and installing AC generators at Niagara Falls, creating the first modern power station.
A: Nikola Tesla

Q: Who developed the general theory of relativity $E=mc2$ on which the atomic bomb is based?
A: Albert Einstein

Q: Who was known for his law on gravitation, invented calculus, explained the theory of tides, and also invented the reflecting telescope?
A: Sir Isaac Newton

Q: Who is the father of modern science because of his discoveries in astronomy and physics?
A: Galileo Galilei

Q: Who explained the 'Germ Theory', created a process of toning and treating milk free from the damage causing microbes he called 'Pasteurization', and discovered a cure for anthrax, puerperal fever, rabies by inventing vaccines?
A: Louis Pasteur

Q: Who patented 1093 inventions in his life time, which include batteries, cement, lights, mining, phonographs, telegraphs, and improved the telephone and was famous for his quote 'Genius is 1% inspiration and 99% perspiration'?
A: Thomas Alva Edison

Q: Who is the first female to be awarded with a Nobel Prize, invented the first mobile X-Ray machine, invented Radium, experimented on elements to check their radio activity, and was called 'the mother of the atom bomb' with her invention of the radio active material?
A: Marie Curie Sklodowska

Q: Who discovered benzene, the principles of electromagnetic induction, diamagnetism, and electrolysis, the system of oxidation numbers, and contributed to the study of electromagnetism and electrochemistry?
A: Michael Faraday

Q: Who is regarded as the greatest mathematician of all time and gave descriptions for the first finite geometric progression, computed areas and volumes of spheres and parabolic segments and is famous for saying 'Give me a place to stand and I can move the world'?
A: Archimedes

Q: Who elaborated and estimated the size of earth and explained the chain of life through his study in flora and fauna, was a biologist, ethicist, zoologist and a political scientist and a master of rhetoric and logic and tutored Alexander the great?
A: Aristotle

AERONAUTICS
(Study of Aircraft & Navigation)

Q: Who invented the airplane?
A: The Wright Brothers

Q: What is the name of the oldest airline? Bonus: What year?
A: KLM Royal Dutch Airlines. Bonus: 1919

Q: What item was removed from each first class salad served on American Airlines in 1987? Bonus: How much did they save?
A: Olive. Bonus: $40,000

Q: How many people on any given hour are airborne over the USA? Bonus: How many people a day?
A: 61,000. Bonus: Over 2 million passengers.

Q: How many flights are flown each day in the USA?
A: 30,000

Q: What is the busiest airport in the world?
Bonus: How many passengers a year?
A: Hartsfield-Jackson Atlanta International Airport.
Bonus: Over 110 million passengers

ANATOMY
(Study of the Parts of Organisms)

Q: What is the largest organ in the human body?
A: Skin

Q: What is the only part of the body that takes oxygen directly from the air?
A: The cornea (the eye)

Q: How much does the average brain weigh?
A: 3.3 lbs

Q: What are the four different brain waves frequencies called?
A: Alpha, Beta, Delta, & Theta

Q: How many neurons in an average brain?
A: 86 million

Q: How many times does your heart beat a day?
A: About 100,000 times

Q: How many cells are in your body?
A: Over 10 trillion cells

Q: How fast is a nerve impulse from the brain?
A: 274 mph

Q: How long is the human intestine?
A: 17 feet

Q: How many miles of blood vessels are there in the human body?
A: 59,650 miles

Q: How many teeth does the adult human have?
A: 32. Bonus Children have 20

Q: What is the largest muscle in the human body? Bonus: Scientific terminology
A: The Buttocks. Bonus: Gluteus Maximus

Q: What is the strongest muscle in the human body?
Bonus: What force does it have?
A: Masseter located on the jaw Bonus: working together with the other jaw muscles to close the teeth with a force of 200 (psi) pounds on the molars.

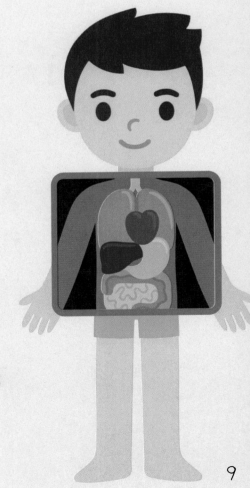

Q: What is the only muscular organ is not attached to skeleton?
A: Tongue

Q: How many taste buds does a human have on their tongue?
A: 10,000

ASTRONOMY (Study of Outer Space) / COSMOLOGY (Study of Universe)

Q: What is the most common element in the Universe?
Bonus: Chemical Symbol.
A: Hydrogen. Bonus: H

Q: Who was the first man to step on the moon?
A: Neil Armstrong

Q: How many planets are in our solar system?
A: Eight

Q: About how many stars are in the Milky Way?
A: 150-250 billion

Q: What color is Mars? Bonus: Why?
A: Red. Bonus: Iron Oxide

Q: Which planet is closest to Earth?
A: Venus (on only part of its orbit).
Bonus Mercury is closest to Earth the longest.

Q: What is the largest planet in our solar system?
A: Jupiter

Q: What planet spins the fastest, completing a rotation in just 10 hours?
A: Jupiter

Q: What planet is the hottest in the solar system?
A: Venus

Q: Which planet in our Solar System is known for having a ring?
A: Saturn

Q: What two planets literally rain diamonds?
A: Jupiter and Saturn

Q: Can you name the closest star to Earth?
A: The sun

Q: How long does it take for light to travel from the Sun's surface to the Earth?
A: 8 minutes and 20 seconds

Q: Which planet has a day that lasts almost eight months on Earth?
A: Venus

Q: What was the first animal to go into orbit? Bonus: Name?
A: A dog. Bonus: What was the name of the dog? Laika

Q: How many Earths can fit inside the sun?
A: 1.3 million

Q: How far is the Moon from Earth in miles?
A: 238,900 mi

BIOLOGY
(Study of Life)

Q: What are the building blocks of life?
A: Cells

Q: Scientist who studies cells is called?
A: Cytologist

Q: How long does a human red blood cell survive?
A: 120 days

Q: Which glands produce white blood cells?
A: Lymph glands

CHEMISTRY
(Study of Atomic Matter)

Q: Who invented the modern periodic table?
A: Dmitri Mendeleyev

Q: How many elements are in the periodic table?
A: 118

Q: Diamonds and Graphite are both made entirely of what element?
A: Carbon, C

Q: What does H2O stand for?
A: Water

Q: What is the essential gas we need to breathe?
Bonus: The Chemical Symbol?
A: Oxygen. Bonus O

Q: Most of a penny is made up of what type of metal?
A: Zinc

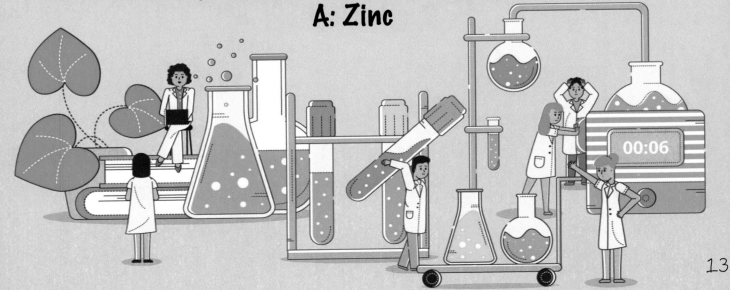

BOTANY
(Study of Plants)

Q: How many plants species are there?
A: Over 300,000

Q: How many species of edible plants are there on Earth?
A: More than 80,000

Q: 90% of the foods humans eat come from how many plants?
A: 30

Q: Medicine utilizes how many different species of plants?
A: 70,000

Q: What percent of plant life is found in the ocean?
A: 85%

Q: The Amazon Rainforest produces what percent of the world's oxygen supply?
A: 50%

Q: What is the name of the tallest tree ever?
Bonus: How tall?
A: Australian Eucalyptus.
Bonus: 435 feet tall!

Q: What is the tallest known living tree?
Bonus: Scientific name?
A: A Sequoia sempervirens redwood
Bonus: Hyperion

Q: The average size tree can make how many pencils?
Bonus: Average height is what?
A: 170,100 pencils. Bonus: 87.6 feet tall.
Bonus 2: 435 feet = 844,674 pencils

Q: Is Cucumber a fruit or vegetable?
Bonus: Why?
A: Fruit.
Bonus: Because it has seeds in the middle

Q: What is the tallest type of grass?
Bonus: How many inches can it grow in a day?
A: Bamboo.
Bonus: 35 inches in a day!

CHROMATICS

Q: What is the most popular color in the world?
Bonus: What percent picked this color?
A: Blue. Bonus: 40% (purple was second at 14%)

Q: What color is a polar bear's skin?
A: Black

Q: What colors in a rainbow order from top to bottom?
A: ROYGBIV: Red, orange, yellow, green, blue, indigo, violet.

Q: What color are the stars in the American flag?
A: White

Q: What is the most popular color of car?
Bonus! What is the 2nd most popular color?
A: White. Bonus: Silver

Q: What color attracts mosquitoes the most?
A: Dark Blue. Instead wear light colored, loose fitting long sleeves.

Q: What is it called if you fear colors?
A: Chromophobia.

Q: What eliminates Black and White
from being considered a color?
A: They do not have specific wavelengths.
Color is a visible light with a specific wavelength.

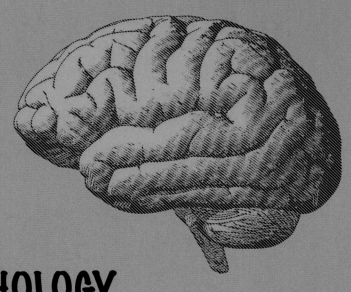

ENCEPHOLOGY
(Study of Brain)

Q: How much does the average brain weigh?
A: 3.3 lbs

Q: What are the four different brain waves frequencies called?
A: Alpha, Beta, Delta, & Theta

Q: How many neurons in an average brain?
A: 86 million

Q: What part of the brain deals with hearing and language?
A: Temporal lobe

ENTOMOLOGY
(Study of Insects)

Q: How many pairs of wings do bees have?
A: Two

Q: How many legs does a spider have?
A: Eight

Q: What animal is considered the best jumper in the world?
Bonus: How high?
A: Flea.
Bonus: 220 times their own body length.

Q: If you have arachnophobia, which animal scares you?
A: Spiders

Q: Which animal kills the most after humans?
Bonus: How many? Bonus 2: What diseases?
A: Mosquito.
Bonus: they afflict an estimated 700 million and kill roughly 725,000 a year. Bonus 2: Malaria, Chikungunya, Dengue Fever, Encephalitis, Elephantiasis, and Yellow Fever.

Q: What color attracts mosquitoes the most?
A: Dark Blue. Instead wear light colored, loose fitting long sleeves.

Q: How can you get African Sleeping Sickness?
Bonus: What happens?
A: Tsetse Fly is a bloodsucking bug.
Bonus: It transmits protozoan parasites that have a neurological and meningoencephalitic symptoms including behavior changes and poor coordination.

GELOTOLOGY
(Study of Laughter)

Q: What chemicals are released from your
brain when you smile?
A: Dopamine, oxytocin, serotonin and endorphins

Q: How many times does the average adult laugh?
A: 15 – 30 times

Q: How many times does the average baby laugh?
A: 300 times

Q: What hormone is released that boosts your
immune system when you laugh?
A: HGH which helps you fight germs.

GENETICS
(Study of Heredity)

Q: Who is the father of genetics?
A: Gregor Mendel

Q: What percent are all humans identical on a genetic level?
A: 99%

GEOLOGY
(Study of Rocks)

Q: What is the hardest natural substance?
A: A diamond

Q: What is the largest granite rock in the world?

Q: What is the largest single stone in the world?
Bonus: How big? Bonus #2: Where?
A: Uluru. Bonus: 1,142 feet. Bonus #2: Ayers Rock, Australia

GEOGRAPHY
(Study of the Earth)

Q: How old is Earth?
A: 4.5 Billion years

Q: Circumference of Earth?
A: 24,901 miles

Q: What are the three layers of Earth?
A: Core, Mantle, and Crust

Q: How fast is Earth spinning through space?
A: Over 1,000 miles per hour

Q: Hottest spot on Earth? Bonus: Other Hot spots?
A: Death Valley, California set the world record of 134° F
was recorded July 10, 2013.
Bonus: Lut Desert, Iran measured 159.3° F 2005
by NASA's Aqua Satellite. Aziziyah, Libya, 136° F degrees
Fahrenheit. 2005

Q: What is the largest living structure on Earth?
A: The Great Barrier Reef world's largest coral reef composed
of over 2900 individual reefs and 900 miles stretching
1,400 miles (and 133,000 sq. mi.). Located in the Coral Sea
off the coast of Queensland, Australia.

Q: Where are the world's most active volcano located?
A: Hawaii

Q: How many continents are there? What are the names?
A: Africa, Antarctica, Asia, Australia, Europe, North America & South America

Q: What is the largest continent?
A: Asia

Q: What is the driest continent?
A: Antartica

Q: What is the largest country in the world?
A: Russia

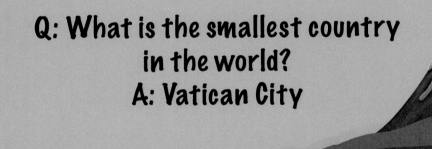

Q: What is the smallest country in the world?
A: Vatican City

Q: What is the largest ocean on Earth?
A: The Pacific

Q: What is the smallest ocean in the world?
A: The Artic

Q: What is the tallest mountain in the world?
A: Mount Everest

Q: What is the longest river in the world?
Bonus: How many miles?
A: The Nile. Bonus: 4,132 miles

Q: What city has the largest population in the world?
Bonus: population. Bonus 2: 2nd, 3rd?
A: Tokyo.
Bonus: 37 million. Delhi – 30 million, Shanghai – 26 million

ICHTHYOLOGY
(Study of Fish)

Q: How many bones do sharks have?
A: Zero

Q: What is the fastest aquatic animal? Bonus: Speed in mph? Bonus 2: Shark & Dolphin mph?
A: The sailfish. Bonus: It can reach speeds of up to 68 mph. Bonus 2: Shark 44 mph, Dolphin 37 mph.

LINGUISTICS & PHILOLOGY
(Study of Languages)

Q: Which continent is the most linguistically diverse in the world? Bonus: How many languages?
A: Africa. Bonus: 800 to 1500 of the world's languages

Q: Which country is the most linguistically diverse in the world? Bonus: How many languages?
A: Africa. Bonus: More than 820 languages

HYDROLOGY
(Study of Water)

Q: What are the three forms of water?
A: Solid, liquid and gas

Q: What temperature does water freeze?
A: 32° F

Q: What temperature does water boil?
A: 212° F

Q: Water has a pH level of around
A: 7

Q: Water is what percent of the human body?
A: 60%

Q: How much of the earth's surface is water?
A: 80%

Q: What percent of earth's water
is ocean and seas?
A: 97%

Q: What percent of earth's water is
frozen and unusable?
A: 2%

Q: What percent of earth's water is
suitable for drinking?
A: 1%

Q: How much water does an individual use daily?
A: Over 100 gallons (all uses)

Q: How much water to the utilities
process daily?
A: 38 billion gallons

MATHEMATICS
(The Study of Numbers)

Q: What is the total if you add up all the numbers from 1 to 100 consecutively (1+2+3...)
A: 5050

Q: How many zeros in a trillion?
A: Twelve zeros

Q: What is the next named number after a trillion?
A: Quadrillion

Q: What does 111,111,111 x 111,111,111 =?
A: 12,345,678,987,654,321

Q: Fibonacci number sequence strongly relates to The Golden Ratio such that each number is the sum of two preceding ones. Starting with 0, 1, 1, 2, 3, 5, 8... next number is?
A: 13

METEOROLOGY
(Study of Weather)

Q: Stratus, cirrus, cumulus and nimbus are types of what?
A: Clouds

Q: What does a thermometer measure?
A: Temperature

Q: During a thunderstorm, which comes first:
lightning or thunder?
A: Both. They occur at approximately the same time.
However, if we're at a distance from a storm,
we see lightning before we hear thunder because light
travels much faster than sound.

MICROBIOLOGY
(Study of Microorganisms)

Q: What is the strongest living creature on Earth?
A: Gonorrhea Bacterium is pound for pound the
strongest living creature on Earth. Capable of pulling up to
100,000 times its own body weight.

NUTRITION
(Study of Food)

Q: Healthiest food in the world?
BONUS: Name 4 more.
A: Spinach.
Bonus: Black Beans, Walnuts, Beets, & Alvocado

Q: What fruit floats because 25% of its volume is air?
A: Apple

Q: What food serves as the base for guacamole?
A: Avocado

Q: What is the only fruit that has its seeds on the outside?
Bonus: How many?
A: Strawberries. Bonus: 200

Q: Where are all the vitamins in a potato?
A: The skin.

Q: What do you eat as a vegetarian?
A: Plant-based foods, like vegetables,
fruits, beans, soy, grains, rice and nuts.

OSTEOLOGY
(Study of Bones)

Q: How many bones in the human body?
A: 206

Q: What bone are babies born without?
A: Kneecap

Q: What is the longest and strongest bone?
A: The Femur

Q: What is the smallest bone in the human body?
Bonus: What are the other two?
A: Stapes located in the Middle ear.
Bonus: Malleus and Incus

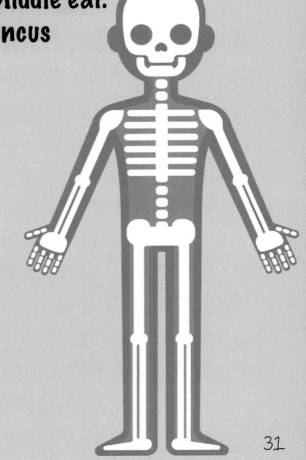

PATHOLOGY
(Study of Disease)

Q: Who discovered a way to treat infections with Penicillin?
A: Alexander Fleming

SCATOLOGY
(Study of Feces 'Poop')

Q: What is bat guano (poop) explosive? Bonus: How was it used?
A: Consists of Potassium Nitrate (Saltpeter). Bonus: It has been harvested for making gunpowder.

Q: What product does the Civet produces?
A: Most expensive coffee beans.

Q: How much paper is produced a day from elephant dung?
A: Elephant dung can produce 100 pages of pager a day (POO-APER)

Q: Which animal is in a constant state of pooping and vomiting? Bonus: Why?
A: House Fly. Bonus: When it eats, it immediately digests and goes right back out. Since the frontal excrements are a way of pre-digesting food before they consume it. If a fly lands on you, it has already pooped and vomited on you.

Q: What animal has a special type of poop that fights pollution? Bonus: Why?
A: Llamas. Bonus: It dilutes acids that comes from mines and also dissolves metals that could be harmful when consumed.

Q: Who left poop on the moon? Bonus: How much poop?
A: Neil Armstrong Bonus: He was kind enough to leave four bags of poop.

Q: What animal poops sand? Bonus: Why?
A: Parrot Fish. Bonus: Because they eat coral with their beaks.

TOXICOLOGY (Study of Poisons)

Q: What is the most violently toxic plant in North America?
A: Water Hemlock (Cicuta Masculata)

Q: What plant was responsible for the death of Abraham Lincoln's mother, Nancy Hanks?
A: White Snakeroot (Ageratina Altissima).
Nancy Hanks was poisoned by simply drinking the milk of a cow that had grazed on the plant.

Q: What plant kills the most people per year?
Bonus: How many die a year?
A: Tobacco (Nicotina tabacum). Bonus: 5 million deaths a year. The leaves contain a toxic alkaloids nicotine and anabasine that can be fatal if eaten. Nicotine is both psychoactive and addictive.

ZOOLOGY
(Study of Animals)

Q: What is the only species living today that
are direct descendants of dinosaurs?
Bonus: What is the name of the dinosaur they come from?
A: Birds. Bonus: Theropod Dinosaurs

Q: Scientist who studies animal behavior is called?
A: Ethologist

Q: What percentage of Animals are extinct?
A: 99%

Q: What percentage of Animals are invertebrates?
A: 95%

Q: What is the fastest land animal? Bonus: Speed in mpg?
A: The Cheetah. They have set record speeds near 70 mph.

Q: What is the largest land animal on Earth?
A: African Elephant

Q: What is the world's largest invertebrate?
A: Giant squid

Q: Which animal is the tallest in the world? Bonus: How tall?
A: Giraffe. Bonus: 15 – 20 feet.

Q: What do you call a group of giraffes?
A: A Tower

Q: Which animal has no vocal cords?
A: Giraffe

Q: What is a group of lions called?
A: A Pride

Q: What is a group of tigers called?
A: An Ambush or Streak

Q: How many hearts does an Octopus have?
A: 3

Q: What can an animal with a prehensile tail do?
A: Ability to Grip

Q: What is the largest animal on Earth? Bonus: Weight?
A: Blue Whale Bonus: Length - 90 ft. and Weighs about 400,000 pounds.

Q: What is the loudest animal on earth? Bonus: How loud?
A: The sperm whale. Bonus: 188 decibels which can reach 500 miles away. These clicks are so powerful in water that they can blow out your eardrums and can actually vibrate a human body to death.

Q: Which mammal lives the longest?
A: Bowhead whale. They can live up to 200 years!

Q: What animal has the strongest bite in the world? Bonus: What is the psi (pressure per inch)
A: Nile Crocodile. Bonus: 5,000psi. Hippo 1,800psi, Jaguar 1,500psi, Shark 1,350psi, Humans are 200psi.

PHYSICS
(Study of Matter & Energy)

Q: What are the building blocks of matter?
A: Atoms

Q: Who was the scientist to propose the three laws of motion
A: Sir Isaac Newton

Q: What is the speed of light (miles per second)?
A: 186,000 miles per second

Q: What is the speed of sound in mph? Bonus: ft./sec.
A: 761 mph Bonus: (1100 ft./ sec.)

PSYCHOLOGY
(Study of Human Behavior)

Q: What is the phenomenon that explains why people will tend to refuse to offer help when other people are present during an emergency?
A: The Bystander Effect

About Kenny

Kenny 'K3' Rochon, III is a 7-year-old boy, Game Changer - Leader. He recently was published as an author, and he is an expert in children's jokes.

When K3 is not telling jokes, he is playing chess with his daddy, learning how to code, playing Minecraft and Nintendo, and even some learning games that challenge his inquisitive and problem-solving mind.

He enjoys math, playing Sudoku, and expanding his vocabulary with his "Kenny's Fortune" word box. Kenny's Future Word Box is a future product he is coming out with the help other children learn the military alphabet and learn positive powerful words. He uses these words to hone up on his skills as a proficient speller so he can win spelling bees.

He has a yellow belt in Tae Kwon Do and practices so he can protect his Mommy (and Daddy) from danger.

Drawing by Stephania Christianson

About Ken Rochon

Ken loves his son Kenny. He enjoys writing a new book every year to celebrate his son's life and to share valuable lessons with him on character, leadership, and success

You can listen to Ken on his radio show Amplified with Ken Rochon, through the VoiceAmerica Influencer Channel on Mondays at 11 AM Eastern, on Itunes or at www.AmplifiedRadioShow.com

This is Ken's 28th book and now his favorite :) He wants to inspire other parents to create a legacy of love with their children through publishing. Ken has created templates that make publishing books more effortless and affordable. (www.PerfectPublishing.com)

Besides playing with his son, Ken loves to travel the world and has been to over 100 countries. He is a world class photographer and enjoys covering the biggest events in the USA (www.BIGeventsUSA.com)

If you are interested in having Ken speak at your school or event, simply connect with him on Facebook or email him at Ken@TheUmbrellaSyndicate.com.

Ken is the co-founder of the Keep Smiling Movement.com. He has co-authored a series of books focused on setting your mindset to be positive. Check out on Amazon the *Keep Smiling – Shift Happens* Series.

He resides in the Baltimore Washington Metropolitan Area with his family.

More of Kenny's Books

More of Kenny's Books

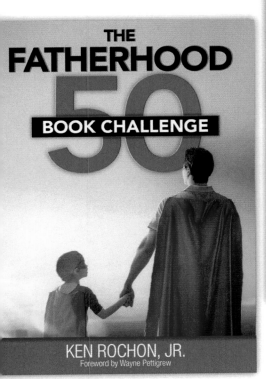

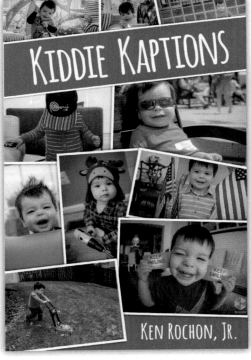

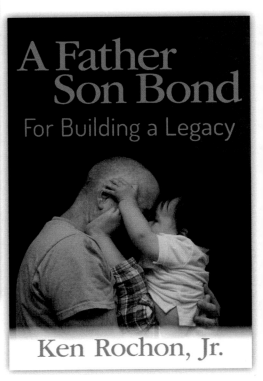

Made in the USA
Middletown, DE
22 June 2021